A Coloring Book for Adults

THE CROSS

And Snowflakes Mandala Patterns

I0454718

Vol.3

Inspired Art Therapy, Flowers and Doodle Style

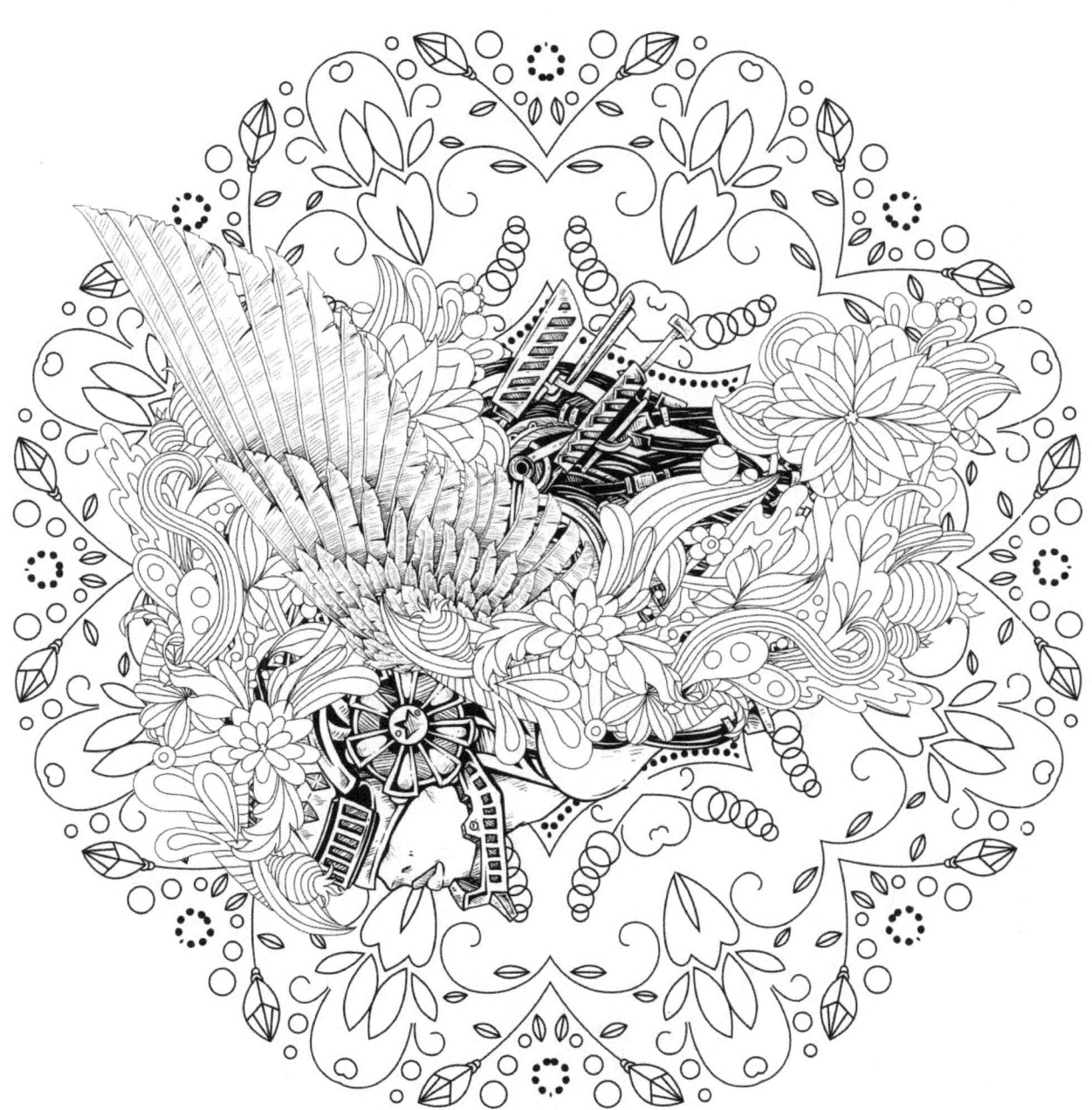

www.ingramcontent.com/pod-product-compliance
Lightning Source LLC
Chambersburg PA
CBHW081855280526
45789CB00007B/2713